DOG DAYS

DOG DAYS

GANDEE VASAN

**Andrews McMeel
Publishing, LLC**

Kansas City

He is my other eyes that can see above the clouds, my other ears that hear above the winds. He is the part of me that can reach out into the sea. He has told me a thousand times over that I am his reason for being: by the way he rests against my leg, by the way he thumps his tail at my smallest smile, by the way he shows his hurt when I leave without taking him. (I think it makes him sick with worry when he is not along to care for me.) When I am wrong, he is delighted to forgive. When I am angry, he clowns to make me smile. When I am happy, he is joy unbounded. When I am a fool, he ignores it. When I succeed, he brags. Without him, I am only another man. With him, I am all-powerful. He is loyalty itself. He has taught me the meaning of devotion. With him, I know a secret comfort and a private peace. He has brought me understanding where before I was ignorant. His head on my knee can heal my human hurts. His presence by my side is protection against my fears of dark and unknown things.

He has promised to wait for me . . . whenever . . . wherever—in case I need him.

And I expect I will—as I always have. He is just my dog.

—Gene Hill

THE BEST MIRROR IS A TRUE FRIEND.

INNOCENT

GUILTY

AMBIVALENT

AMBITIOUS

SAD

BAD

CANNY

CURIOUS

COIFFED

COMPANIONABLE

CUTE

COMPOSED

CONSTRAINED

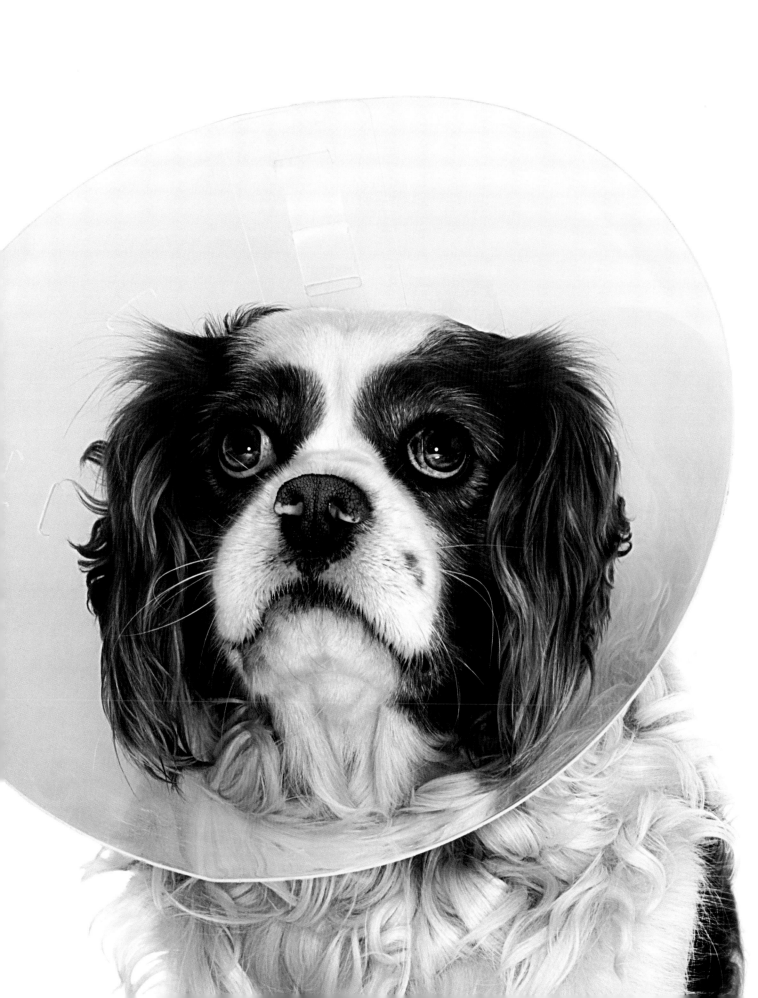

DESPONDENT

DEMURE

DEVOTED

DEFEATED

DISTANT

DISARMING

DISHEVELED

DELICIOUS

DOWN

LEFT

RIGHT

LEFT BEHIND

NAGGING

NAGGED

BRAVE

BEAUTIFUL

BIG

SMALL

BEHOLDEN

BEHIND

GRUFF

ROUGH

TOUGH

FLUFF

ALERT

ALOOF

ADORABLE

WAITING

WORRIED

WIRED

WINDSWEPT

WISE

WEARY

HAIRY

HAIRIER

HAIRIEST

PERT

PATIENT

PERMED

PERPLEXED

DAZED

CONFUSED

BLACK

SHORT

HUMBLE

HOPEFUL

HONORABLE

OBEDIENT

O V E R   I T

UNDER IT

EARNEST

EXPECTANT

ERRATIC

ENVIOUS

ENDLESS

LEAN

LOVABLE

LINKED

LONGING

LAST

Dog Days began with our family pet, Basil. Basil is a golden retriever and the joy of our lives.

My wife takes Basil to a dog grooming salon called Top Dogs to have him washed. My view was that the money spent was money wasted when Basil could have been hosed down in the garden. However, this changed the day my wife asked me to collect Basil from the salon. The lineup of dogs being groomed had me utterly enthralled. Their expressions as they were being blow-dried, and the pain on their faces as the comb got stuck in their hair was, well, very human. More human than human: caricatures of human faces, with an endearing "dogginess" thrown in.

Fascinated, I asked Beverly, the owner of Top Dogs, if I could spend a day photographing the dogs. It really was intriguing to see how nonchalant the dogs remained as they had all their hair shaved off, stood in the sink shivering, or casually held up their feet to have their nails clipped.

When I looked at the pictures I had taken that day I realized that to capture the images I was really after I needed the dogs to come to the studio, and that trained dogs would be required. I spent two days in a studio shooting twenty dogs—trained pedigrees this time, accompanied by their handlers. They were surprisingly obliging, at times posing just as humans would. In true doggy fashion, however, their great motivator was food, and a variety of sounds.

Although one can never be sure, I had a good feeling about the series of pooch portraits I'd taken in those two days. The images won awards in London and New York and were published in *Photo District News* magazine . . . which is what eventually led to the publication of this book.

What I hadn't quite registered when embarking on the book was how important it was to capture a great variety of images and a great variety of dog breeds. Lots of different dogs: short dogs and tall dogs, plump and thin, wrinkled and smooth, cute and cuddly.

Having started my career as a portrait painter, what I've always found fascinating about people is how different everyone is. Well, dogs, just in their looks—the range, the different types of hair, of skin, of expressions, and of attitudes—have a thousand times more variety.

I am very fortunate because Britain is of course a nation of dog lovers, and therefore the perfect place to photograph a multitude of dogs! I see dogs everywhere: when I'm driving my son to football and stop at the traffic lights, a French bulldog in the backseat of the next car stares back with saliva dribbling out of its mouth; when I go shopping in the local corner shop a little spaniel waits anxiously for its owner. Sometimes I think there are more dogs than people in England.

To source as great a variety of breeds and doggy characters as possible for *Dog Days* I made leaflets explaining what we were doing and asked dog owners to bring their dogs to my studio. My wife distributed the leaflets at the local park, Beverly at Top Dogs handed them out to owners visiting the salon, I left them at Goddards, the local vets. The leaflets were a success—we ended up shooting about seventy dogs in a six-week period.

You know what they say about dogs mirroring their owners—that's exactly what I first noticed when I saw the owners arriving with their dogs. I had a wonderful Hungarian puli who looked just like a mop with legs thanks to his Rastafarian hairstyle. I'm not quite sure how he could see, and the only clue as to whether a face was hidden in there or not was his tongue! Interestingly, the owners, also Hungarian, reflected their dog, even in their aroma . . . I'm not sure if it was the smell of the owners rubbing off on the dog or the other way around. There was one woman whose bearing reflected exactly the grace and poise of her elegant poodle, and a Dutch woman who had eyes just like her Siberian husky's. Another woman who came in had a coat very similar to her dog's. Do dogs affect their owners' dress sense, too?

What was extremely touching, without exception, was how attached the owners were to their dogs. There seemed to be an almost telepathic connection between man's best friend and his master, and the dogs were without doubt full members of the family. The dogs also seemed to have a therapeutic effect on their owners.

As it happened, I often got *the* shot as soon as the dogs walked into the studio. They tended to get quickly distracted after that as soon as they figured out what was going on. I was amused by some of the clownlike qualities of the animals. What was intriguing was how the smaller dogs tended to have a cheekiness and an endearing arrogance and chutzpah. They were also very frisky and bold on the shoots. The big dogs tended to be pretty laid-back, imperious and slow, reflecting their bulkiness. The more I looked at all these pooch faces the more I wondered why people don't have faces like dogs and not the other way around; they just have so much character. Some dogs sauntered into the studio as if they owned the place, others took gentle steps as if on a narrow footbridge; some had the march of a sergeant, others, like the black poodle Shadow, the delicate steps of a ballerina. Some were straining at the leash to get out of the studio; others made themselves at home and settled down to feast on the treats we supplied to persuade them to pose.

The question I am left with is: Will I ever now find a human face as interesting as a dog's?

GANDEE VASAN

IDENTIFICATION
[DOG BREEDS]

ACKNOWLEDGMENTS

Thank you so much to all the dogs and the dog owners. Every single owner was punctual and took great pleasure in bringing their dogs to me—and what great "sitters" the dogs were. I express gratitude with every picture.

To Beverly Pinch at Top Dogs Grooming for finding all the weird and wonderful dogs; to our local vet's office, Goddards, and everyone there who encouraged clients to bring their dogs to me; to Rehman Nizam, whom I can't thank enough for helping me for many days and long nights finishing off the pictures (and for taking the author portrait of me); Joanne Craske, Neil Fox, and Helena Karlsson for assisting with the photography; to my understanding wife, Anna, and our special children, Misha and Veena, for their suggestions and for tolerating all the long hours I spent without seeing them (and an extra thank-you to Veena for her photograph of Basil); and to Basil, without whom this project would never have started—there are going to be so many walks on the way for you, Basil!

Thank you so much to Geoff Blackwell and Ruth Hobday for spotting my work and seeing the potential in it, and for encouraging me to come up with all these pictures to turn into a book, and to Caroline Bowron for her constant communication and making sense of all my jumbled pictures and words. Thank you to all the people at PQ Blackwell who worked on the book design.

This edition published by Andrews McMeel Publishing, LLC, an Andrews McMeel Universal company, 4520 Main Street, Kansas Ciy, Missouri 64111.

ISBN-13: 978-0-7407-6919-1
ISBN-10: 0-7407-6919-7
Library of Congress Control Number: 2007923207

Produced and originated by PQ Blackwell Limited
116 Symonds Street, Auckland, New Zealand
www.pqblackwell.com

The publishers would like to thank Getty Images for their assistance.

The publisher is grateful for literary permissions to reproduce those items subject to copyright. Every effort has been made to trace the copyright holders, and the publisher apologizes for any unintentional omission. We would be pleased to hear from any not acknowledged here and undertake to make all reasonable efforts to include the appropriate acknowledgment in any subsequent editions.

www.andrewsmcmeel.com

Designed by Carolyn Lewis

Printed by Everbest Printing International Limited, China